HAL•LEONARD
INSTRUMENTAL
PLAY-ALONG

AUDIO
ACCESS
INCLUDED

PLAYBACK+
Speed • Pitch • Balance • Loop

VIOLIN

Disney
Aladdin

T0070963

Audio arrangements by Peter Deneff

To access audio visit:
www.halleonard.com/mylibrary
Enter Code
4747-7241-0848-6276

ISBN 978-1-5400-6241-3

HAL•LEONARD®

Visit Hal Leonard Online at
www.halleonard.com

Contact us:
Hal Leonard
7777 West Bluemound Road
Milwaukee, WI 53213
Email: info@halleonard.com

In Europe, contact:
Hal Leonard Europe Limited
42 Wigmore Street
Marylebone, London, W1U 2RN
Email: info@halleonardeurope.com

In Australia, contact:
Hal Leonard Australia Pty. Ltd.
4 Lentara Court
Cheltenham, Victoria, 3192 Australia
Email: info@halleonard.com.au

Contents

ARABIAN NIGHTS
(2019)

VIOLIN

Music by ALAN MENKEN
Lyrics by HOWARD ASHMAN,
BENJ PASEK and JUSTIN PAUL

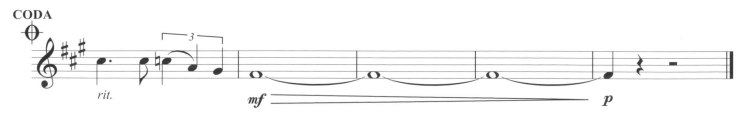

ONE JUMP AHEAD

Violin

Music by ALAN MENKEN
Lyrics by TIM RICE

FRIEND LIKE ME

VIOLIN

Music by ALAN MENKEN
Lyrics by HOWARD ASHMAN

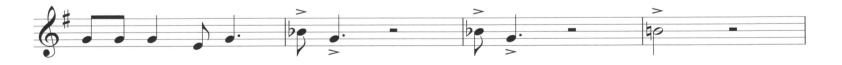

PRINCE ALI

VIOLIN

Music by ALAN MENKEN
Lyrics by HOWARD ASHMAN

Slower, accelerating gradually

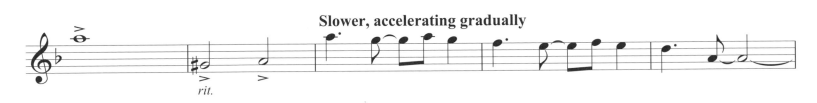

SPEECHLESS

VIOLIN

Music by ALAN MENKEN
Lyrics by BENJ PASEK
and JUSTIN PAUL

Moderately

A WHOLE NEW WORLD

VIOLIN

Music by ALAN MENKEN
Lyrics by TIM RICE